Frozen River
(nîkwatin sîpiy)

Frozen River
(nîkwatin sîpiy)

Michaela Washburn, Joelle Peters,
and Carrie Costello

Playwrights Canada Press
Toronto

Jacket design by Doowah Design Inc., and provided courtesy of the Manitoba Theatre for Young People
Michaela Washburn author photo © Denise Grant
Joelle Peters author photo © Gaetz Photography

Playwrights Canada Press
202-269 Richmond St. w., Toronto, ON M5V 1X1
416.703.0013 | info@playwrightscanada.com | www.playwrightscanada.com

For professional or amateur production rights, please contact Playwrights Canada Press.

LIBRARY AND ARCHIVES CANADA CATALOGUING IN PUBLICATION
Title: Frozen river = Nîkwatin sîpiy / Michaela Washburn, Joelle Peters, & Carrie Costello.
Other titles: Nîkwatin sîpiy
Names: Washburn, Michaela, author. | Peters, Joelle, author. | Costello, Carrie, author.
Description: First edition. | In English, with some text in Nehiyaw.
Identifiers: Canadiana (print) 20230592511 | Canadiana (ebook) 2023059252X | ISBN 9780369104892 (softcover) | ISBN 9780369104908 (PDF) | ISBN 9780369104915 (EPUB)
Subjects: LCGFT: Drama.
Classification: LCC PS8645.A82 F76 2024 | DDC C812/.6—dc23

Playwrights Canada Press staff work across Turtle Island, on Treaty 7, Treaty 13, and Treaty 20 territories, which are the current and ancestral homes of the Anishinaabe Nations (Ojibwe / Chippewa, Odawa, Potawatomi, Algonquin, Saulteaux, Nipissing, and Mississauga / Michi Saagiig), the Blackfoot Confederacy (Kainai, Piikani, and Siksika), néhiyaw, Sioux, Stoney Nakoda, Tsuut'ina, Wendat, and members of the Haudenosaunee Confederacy (Mohawk, Oneida, Onondaga, Cayuga, Seneca, and Tuscarora), as well as Métis and Inuit peoples. It always was and always will be Indigenous land.

We acknowledge the financial support of the Canada Council for the Arts, the Ontario Arts Council (OAC), Ontario Creates, the Government of Ontario, and the Government of Canada for our publishing activities.

From the Playwrights

The three of us share the desire to challenge our audiences of young people to think about big issues in meaningful ways, knowing that small things in young lives can have *big* effects throughout the next seven generations. For many folks, the first experience of live theatre is often in school. In writing for this age range, you need to honour the intelligence of children and respect their honest responses to the work. It is important for us to create relevant and intelligent stories that young people can identify with as well as to create work that young people feel empowered by when they are exposed to it, both in terms of story and career possibilities.

In the writing process we were grappling with the very issues that we were trying to portray for our young audiences. What does reconciliation mean? How do we leave audiences with hope? Do *we* still have hope? After hearing the responses to *Frozen River* from many students, teachers, and fellow artists, the answer is yes, we still have hope. And the future is in good hands.

Language Notes

Throughout the script **bolded text** indicates Swampy Cree and Scots Gaelic. Please refer to the table below for more details on pronunciation. If you are reading this script for the first time, you may skip these language tables as there are translations throughout the text.

Language: maskêko-ininîmowin [Swampy Cree language]

Please note that capitals are not used in this language unless it is a name. We are very grateful to our Language Keeper Cameron Robertson for his unfailing support of this project. We have chosen to keep the language in an older form because of the time period of most of the play. Some of the syllabics have been written for ease of phonetic pronunciation. For access to language support and recordings please contact the playwrights.

English	Syllabics	Written	Phonetic
Frozen River	ᓃᐧᑲᑎᐣ ᓰᐲ	nîkwatin sîpiy	ni-kwa-tin see-pee
Grand-mother Moon	ᑯᐦᑰᒥᓇᓂᐤᐲᓯᒼ	Kohkôminawipîsim	koh-koo-mi-naa-wi pee-sim
Blood Moon	ᒥᐦᑯᐧᐃᐲᓯᒼ	mihkowi-pîsim	mih-ko-wi pee-sim
her/their grandmother	ᐅᐦᑯᒪ	Ohkoma	ooh-koo-maa
What are you looking at, my child?	ᑫᐧᑲᐣ ᑳ ᑳᓇᐧᐊᐸᐦᑕᒫᐣ, ᓂᒐᐧᐊᓯᒥᐢ?	kêkwan kâ kânawapahtamân, nicawasimis	ke-kwan kaa-ka-na-pah-ta-maan, ni-tsa-wa-si-mis

Okânawâpacikêw	ᐆᑳᓇᐧᐋᐸᒋᑫᐤ	Okânawâpacikêw	o-kaa-na-waa-pa-tsi-kew
the Meeting Place	ᐃᑕ ᑳ ᒫᐧᐊᒌᑐᓈᓂᐧᐊᐠ	ita kâ mâwacîtonâniwâk	i-ta kaa maa-wa-tsi-to-naa-ni-waak
Swampy Cree	ᒪᐢᑫᑯᐃᓂᓂᐧᐊᐠ	maskêko-ininiwak	ma-ske-ko In-in-e-wak
Gathering of Peoples	ᒪᒫᐧᐊᒋᐦᐃᑐᐧᐃᐣ	mâmâwacîhitowin	maa-maa-wa-tsi-hi-to-win
where Great Spirit sits	ᐃᑕ ᑭᐦᒋᒪᓂᑐ ᑳ ᐊᔭᐱᐟ	ita Kihci-Manito kâ âyapit	ita Kih-tsi ma-ni-to kaa a-ya-pit
sorry I was just—	ᒉᐢᐧᑲ ᒣᐧᑳᐨ ᐅᒪ	cêskwa, mêkwâc oma	tse-skwa, mey-kwaa-ts oma
water	ᓂᐲᐩ	nipîy	ni-pee
Water. Drink.	ᓂᐲᐩ᙮ ᒥᓂᐧᑫ᙮	nipîy. minikwê.	ni-pee. mi-ni-kwey
Where are you going?	ᑕᓂᑕ ᐃᑐᐦᑌᔮᐣ	tanita itohtêyân	ta-ni-ta itoh-tey-yan
You shouldn't be out here by yourself.	ᐧᒫᐨ ᐅᑕ ᑲᑮ ᐹᐯᔭᑰᔭᐣ᙮	mwâc ota kakî pâpêyakôyan	mwa-ts ota ka-kee paa-pey-ya-koo-yan
Eat.	ᒦᒋᓯᐤ	mîcisiw	me-tsi-siw
No! Poisonous.	ᐧᒫᐨ! ᑳᐱᐢᒋᐴᐣ	mwâc! piscipowin.	mwa-ts pis-tsi-po-win
Poisonous. *(more urgent)*	ᐱᐢᒋᐳᐧᐃᓂᐧᐃᐣ	piscipowiniwin	pis-tsi-po-wini-win
See. The leaves are different. You need to look.	ᐧᐋᐸᐦᑕ᙮ ᓂᐱᔭ ᑲᐦᑭᓇᐤ ᒦᐢᑯᒋᓇᑰᓯᐧᐊᐠ᙮ ᒌᐢᐟᑲᓇᐧᐊᐸᐦᑕ᙮	wâpahta. nîpîya kahkînaw mîsko-cinakôsiwak. cîst-kanawapahta.	waa-pah-ta. nee-pee-ya kah-ki-naw mee-sko-tsi-na-koo-si-wak. tsee-st kah-na-wa-pah-ta.
And this one?	ᐆᒪ ᒫ?	ôma mâ	oo-ma maa
Yes!	ᑕᐧᐯ!	tapwê	ta-pwey
No. That way.	ᐧᒫᐨ᙮ ᓀᑌ ᐃᓯ᙮	mwâc. nêtê isi.	mwaa-ts. ney-tey isi.

The one who speaks many languages, he/she knows yours, and we can find out why you are alone in the woods.	ᐊᓇ ᒥᐦᓰᐟ ᐱᑭᐢ ᐎᐧᐁᐎᓇ ᑳ ᐊᔮᒥᐟ, ᑭᐢᑫᓂᐦᑕᒼ ᑳ ᐃᓯ ᐊᔮᒥᔮᐣ, ᐁᐧᑲ ᑲᑭ ᑭᐢᑫᓂᑕᐤ ᑫᑿᐣ ᐅᐦᒋ ᐯᔭᑯᔮᐣ ᐅᑕ ᓅᐦᒋᒥᕽ	ana mihcêt pîkisk-wêwina kâ âyamit, kiskênihtâm kâ isi âyamiyân, êkwa kakî kiskênit-naw kêkwan ohci pêyakoyân ota nôhcimihk.	ana mih-tset pee-kis-kwey-wina kaa a-ya-mit, kis-keh-nih-taa-m kaa isi aya-mee-yan, ek-wa ka-ki kis-keh-ni-tey-naw kee-kwan oh-tsi pey-ya-ko-yan ota noo-tci-mihk.
my family	ᓂ ᐊᐧᐦᑰᒫᑳᓇᐠ	ni wahkômâkânak	ni-wah-koo-maa-kaa-nak
your family	ᓂ ᐊᐧᐦᑰᒫᑳᓇᐠ	ki wahkômâkânak	ki-wah-koo-maa-kaa-nak
family (please note this is not proper language use without the "ki" or "ni" or something else in front of it)	ᓂ ᐊᐧᐦᑰᒫᑳᓇᐠ	wahkômâkânak	wah-koo-maa-kaa-nak
Okay. I know this place. Let's go.	ᐦᐊᐤ ᓂᑭᐢᑫᓂᑕᐣ ᐃᑕ ᐁᐧᑲ ᒫᑲ	hâw. nikiskênitân ita. êkwa mâka.	haaw. ni-kis-keh-ni-taan it-a. ehk-wa maa-ka.
You have done well, Okânawâpacikêw.	�kᐃᐧᔭᐢᐠ ᑭᑐᑕᐣ, ᐅᑳᓇᐊᐧᐸᒋᑫᐤ	kwâyask kitotân, Okânawâpacikêw.	kwaa-yask ki-to-tane, Okaa na-waa-pa-tsi kew.
Hello my child. You have arrived in the world in a good way.	ᑕᓂᓯ ᓂᒐᐊᐧᓯᒥᐢ ᑳ ᒥᓄᑕᑯᓯᓂᐣ ᐊᐢᑮᕽ	tanisi nicawasimis. kâ minotakosinin askîhk.	ta-ni-si ni-tsa-wa-si-mis. kaa mino-ta-ko-si-nin ask-ee-hk.
You are welcome.	ᑮᓇ ᐅᐦᒋ ᐳᑯ ᒫᓂᒫᑲ	kîna ohci poko mânimâka.	kee-na oh-tsi po-ko maa-ni-maa-ka.
Wâpam	ᐋᐧᐸᒼ	Wâpam	Waa-pam
moose	ᒨᓴ	môswa	moo-swa
rabbit		wapôs	Wa-poo-s
thank you	ᐁᑯᓴᓂ	êkosanî	e-ko-sa-nee

one two three four five six seven eight nine ten eleven twelve	ᐯᔭᐠ ᓃᓱ ᓂᐢᑐ ᓀᐓ ᓃᔮᓇᐣ ᓂᑯᐛᓯᐠ ᑌᐸᑯᐦᑊ ᐊᔦᓈᓀᐤ ᑫᑳ-ᒥᑖᑕᐦᐟ ᒥᑖᑕᐦᐟ ᐯᔭᑯᓵᑊ ᓃᓱᓵᑊ	pêyak nîso nisto nêwo nîyânan nikotwâsik têpakohp ayênânêw kêkâc-mitâtaht mitâtaht pêyakosâp nîsosâp	pey-ak nee-siw nis-to ney-wo nee-yaa-nan ni-ko-twaa-sik tey-pa-kohp aye-enaa-nehw kay-kaa-ts mi- taa-ta-ht mi-taa-ta-ht pey-ak-o-sap nee-siw-sap
during a blood moon	ᒥᐦᑯᐏᐲᓯᒨᐦᐠ ᐃᐢᐲᐦᐠ	mihkowi-pîsimôhk ispîhk	mih-ko-wi pee-sim-oo-hk is-pee-hk
red	ᒥᐦᑯᐤ	mihkow	mih-kow
moon	ᑎᐱᐢᑲᐏᐲᓯᒼ	tipiskawi-pîsim	ti-pi-ska-wi pee-sim
medicines	ᒪᐢᑭᐦᑮ	maskihkî	ma-skih-kee
cranberries	ᒪᐢᑫᑯᒥᓈᓇ	maskêkominâna	ma-skey-ko- mi-naa-na
the one who speaks many languages	ᐊᓇ ᒥᐦᒉᐟ ᐲᑭᐢᑵᐏᓇ ᑳ ᐊᔭᒥᐟ, ᑭᐢᑫᓂᐦᑖᒪᐠ ᑲ ᐃᓯ ᐊᔭᒦᔫ, ᐁᑿ ᑲᑭ ᑭᐢᑫᓂᑌᓇᐤ ᑫᒁᐣ	ana mihcet pîkisk- wêwina kâ ayamit.	ana mih-tset pee- kis-kwey-wina kaa a-ya-mit
early fall freeze-up winter early spring spring	ᐑᐸᐨ ᑕᒁᑭᐣ ᐊᑎ ᐋᐦᑿᑎᐣ ᐱᐳᐣ ᐑᐸᐨ ᐯ ᓲᑿᐣ ᑳ ᓲᒁᐦᐠ᙮	wîpac takwâhkin ati âhkwatin pipon wîpac pê sîkwan kâ sîkwâhk	wee-pats ta- kwaah-kin ati aah-kwa-tin pi-pon wee-pats pay see-kwan ka see-kwaa'hk
little one (child)	ᓂᒐᐘᓯᒥᐢ	nicawasimis	ni-tsa-wa-si-mis
his/her family	ᐆᑎᐱᓇᐍ ᐘᐦᑯᒪᑲᓈᐠ	ô wahkomakanâk	oo wah-ko- ma-ka-nak
Eagle Moon (February)	ᒥᑭᓯᐏᐱᓯᒼ	mikisiwi-pîsim	mi-ki-si-wi pee-sim
Falling Leaf Moon (October)	ᐱᓈᐢᑲᐏᐲᓯᒼ	pinâskawi-pîsim	pi-naa-ska-wi pee-sim
sleep	ᓂᐸ	nipa	ni [neh]-pa

my grandmother	ᓄᑲᒻ	Nohkôm	noh-koom
my grandfather	ᓂᒧᓱᒼ	Nimosôm	ni-mo-soom
food stuck in teeth	ᑲ ᓭᑯᑖᐱᑌ	kâ sêkotâpitêt	kaa sey-ko-taa-pi-tate
good morning, Turtle	ᑕᐻ ᒥᓄᐊᐸᐣ, ᒥᓄᐹ	tapwê mino-wapan, o wîtimik-wânisiw	tap-wey mino wa-pan, oh we-ti-mi-kwa-ni-siw
Turtle (the "o" in front endears or individualizes)	ᐅᐱᑎᒧᑲᓂᓯᐤ	o wîtimikwânisiw (translated into old Cree)	oh we-ti-mi-kwa-ni-siw

Language: Scottish Gaelic

We are grateful to our translator Joyce MacDonald from the Gaelic College, St. Ann's, Nova Scotia. Please contact the playwrights for access to the recordings.

English	Scots Gaelic	Phonetic	Recording #
Eilidh	Eilidh	AY-lee, where the "ay" rhymes with "day."	
What are you trying to do, my dearie?	Dè tha thu feuchainn ri dhèanamh, m'eudail?		Gaelic phrases.mp4
grandmother	seanmhair		Gaelic phrases.mp4

Frozen River (nîkwatin sîpiy) was first produced by Manitoba Theatre for Young People and Castlemoon Theatre in February, 2022, with the following cast and creative team:

Grandmother Moon: Krystle Pederson
Okânawâpacikêw (Wâpam): Kathleen MacLean
Eilidh: Mallory James
Eilidh Understudy: RobYn Slade

Directors: Ann Hodges and Tracey Nepinak
Language Keeper: Cameron Robertson
Dialect Coach: Rhea Rodych-Rasidescu
Sets and Props Designer: Andrew Moro
Assistant Set Designer: Shauna Jones
Costume Designer: Jay Havens
Assistant Costume Designer: Amy McPherson
Lighting Designer: Dean Cowieson
Composer and Sound Designer: MJ Dandeneau
Stage Manager: Katie Schmidt

Manitoba Theatre for Young People subsequently toured the production across Canada in 2022 and 2023 with Director Katie German. The two remounts included both original and new cast members. New cast members included Keely McPeek, Julia Davis, and Emily Meadows with Julia Cirillo as the Stage Manager.

Characters

EILIDH: A young Scottish girl; the name means "sun—radiant."

OKÂNAWÂPACIKÊW (WÂPAM): A young **maskêko-ininiwak** [Swampy Cree] person; the name means "one who sees." This name is shortened to "Wâpam," which means "look at them."

MOON: Is herself and ageless. She remains the constant in the world. Moving through her phases and cycles. Sometimes fast, sometimes slow, and sometimes so subtle during the text that we don't clock her disappearance. And when it's a new moon, we only hear her. The effect of her voice and energy should feel cradling to the whole audience, as well as the characters, which she sees as her grandchildren.

The actor playing the moon also takes on the characters of nature/animals/father/Struana.

Setting

The set is the moon. Wâpam and Eilidh do not see the actor playing the moon. The play takes place in Kihci-Manito kâ ayapit, which is in the Red River Valley, in what is now called Manitoba, Canada. Acts One and Two take place after 1837 and before the flood of 1852. Act Three takes place in the present day, during February.

Act One
The River Flows

Scene One: Adventures!

We hear sounds of innovation: videos, a telephone, a radio, a boat; all of which die away and finally, water. We explore the different sounds and landscapes involving water and environments of Manitoba's past.

MOON: I remember. I remember because it was a time before telephones, before radios, when a boat was the only car, and the river was the only road. It was like that for a long time, until one day it wasn't. Who am I? I answer to many things . . . I have many names. Many call me simply the Moon. Some say Wolf Moon. Or Eagle Moon. Falling Leaf Moon . . . But me, I like **Kohkôminawipîsim**. Grandmother Moon. That name suits me just fine.

We witness the evolution of the lunar eclipse that creates a blood moon, and the entire moon turns a soft red colour.

I remember because I was red. I was known as **mihkowi-pîsim**, a Blood Moon. And under this blood moon, a baby was born, hands and feet busy with excitement.

> *The* MOON *engages with the baby on the screen who is held by a Scottish grandmother. The baby moves, trying to reach for the moon with hands and feet.*

Dè tha thu feuchainn ri dhèanamh, m'eudail? *[Gaelic: What are you trying to do, my dearie?]* "What are you trying to do?" her **seanamhair** *[Gaelic: grandmother]* asked. What the little one was trying to do, was to catch me. The baby reached for me, not knowing how far away I was. "You are Eilidh."

Eilidh. I remember. Because this baby did not cry. And not because it couldn't or because there's anything wrong with crying, but because in the glow of my gentle red light, the child was busy trying to do.

On that very same night of the blood moon, across a salty sea, down a winding river, another baby was born.

> *The* MOON *engages with the baby who is held by their grandmother. The baby stares and squints at the* MOON *as though looking to recognize someone or something.*

That baby stared up from the arms of their **Ohkoma** *[grandmother]* with such intention, such focus. **kêkwan kâ kânawapahtamân, nicawasimis?** *[What are you looking at, little one?]* "What are you trying to see?" the baby's **Ohkoma** asked. What the little one was trying to see, was me. **Ohkoma** smiled, as the baby's name suddenly came to her. **Okânawâpacikêw.** "You are **Okânawâpacikêw.**" Ah, I remember because this baby also did not cry. And not because it couldn't or because there's anything wrong with crying, but because in the glow of my gentle red light, the child was busy seeing.

We see the way of life of the Swampy Cree with
OKÂNAWÂPACIKÊW.

Okânawâpacikêw grew up traveling the land of the maple, the spruce, the poplar, the birch, and the willow. The land that stretched between **ita kâ mâwacîtonâniwâk**, the Meeting Place at the two rivers, and way up to the thick forests of the North. They learned the ways of the **maskêko-inin-iwak**. The Swampy Cree. They learned to snare rabbits and squirrels, catch fish, and make birch bark containers for carrying water and berries. They were taught how to harvest the berries and how to look for plants: learning the difference between safe ones to use for teas and medicines, and which ones were poisonous. Their family did not stay in one place for very long. **Okânawâpacikêw** learned to trade at the **mâmâwacîhitowin**, the Gathering of Peoples, which always came during the time when the sun is at its warmest and the leaves haven't yet changed their colours.

During this speech we see the way of life of Scottish farmers
with EILIDH.

Meanwhile far away, Eilidh grew up on the bright green mountains of the Scottish Highlands; home to the sycamore, the Scot's pine, the Birnam oak and the silver birch. Eilidh learned how to farm and cook according to the ways of her people. Her favourite meals always included tatties and neeps . . . you might call them potatoes and turnips. Eilidh's father showed her how to harvest them. From as early as she could walk, Eilidh was busy gathering and making, rarely content to be still. At the age of ten, her family's farm was burnt to the ground, and they could no longer live there. They had very little choice but to leave Scotland in search of a new land.

*EILIDH fidgets with her hands as she sits on a York boat.
She pulls out her collection of birch bark strips and begins
sketching.*

Eilidh's family traveled for many moons across the sea,
across the ocean, and up the original highways of river. They
traveled till they arrived at the land of the maple, the spruce,
the poplar, the birch, and the willow.

*The environment changes, settling on the forest along the
bank of the Red River, just down from Lake Winnipeg.*

To this place. The land was known to Eilidh as Rupert's Land
and to **Okânawâpacikêw** as **ita Kihci-Manito kâ âyapit**
[where Great Spirit sits]. It is a land that might be known to you
now as Manitoba, Canada.

*The MOON takes leaves from the trees and they fall to the
ground.*

The leaves were getting ready to fall from the trees and make
a blanket for the earth in time for freeze-up and in prepara-
tion for winter. I remember.

Scene Two: Gesture of Friendship

*WÂPAM nimbly pops their head out and glances out over the
audience and then returns to their work.*

MOON: **Okânawâpacikêw** has been spending time amongst
the trees practising setting different snares to help their
family stay fed. They must stay very still and keep hidden so
they don't scare away the animals.

The MOON snaps a twig and WÂPAM pops their head out.
They are listening and looking, trying to see. They stay very
still as EILIDH enters a small clearing, tired and thirsty.
The MOON takes a few leaves from the trees and swirls them
around EILIDH, who swats them away tiredly. EILIDH wrestles
to undo the lid of her water bag. Excitedly, she goes to take
a big swig. It's empty. WÂPAM disappears.

EILIDH: Noo!

EILIDH desperately tries to coax out one more drop but to no
avail. EILIDH holds the water bag above her head and emp-
ties it towards her mouth. WÂPAM emerges to sneakily leave
water in a birch bark container on a stump and then hides
again. EILIDH starts trudging forward and does not notice
the water. The MOON rustles some leaves and EILIDH turns,
seeing the container with water on the stump.

Hello?

EILIDH looks about. She puts down her pack.

Hello?

EILIDH pokes at the water container but decides she cannot
risk it and walks away. WÂPAM sneaks back in and grabs the
container. The MOON snaps a series of twigs making EILIDH
turn around and back up.

Hello?

EILIDH notices the water is gone, she looks around. The MOON
snaps a twig behind her.

Who's there?

*WÂPAM puts the container back on the stump and hides
again. EILIDH turns around and sees the water back there.*

What?

*She looks confused. She sniffs the water, almost drinking it
but leaves and continues walking.*

*WÂPAM enters and picks up the water container. They notice
EILIDH's pack, or rather the drawing that is sticking out of it.
WÂPAM inspects the drawing. The MOON snaps a twig. WÂPAM
panics and can't figure out what to do with the drawing
in their hands. They end up hiding with it just as EILIDH
re-enters.*

Right.

*She sighs and picks up her pack. She goes to pull out her
drawing and realizes she can't find it.*

Now where . . . ?

*She looks inside the pack then on the ground. She gets closer
to WÂPAM who tries to leave quietly, but the MOON dumps
a branch full of leaves on WÂPAM, the movement catching
EILIDH's eye. She takes a step back. EILIDH and WÂPAM both
stare at each other fearfully for a moment.*

Who are you?

She notices the drawing in WÂPAM's hands.

Wait, that's mine.

WÂPAM: cêskwa, mêkwâc oma— *[Sorry, I was just—]*

EILIDH: Give it back!

EILIDH holds out her hand and WÂPAM gives back the drawing. WÂPAM offers the water.

WÂPAM: nipîy. *[Water.]*

EILIDH: Water?

WÂPAM: nipîy. minikwê. *[Water. Drink.]*

WÂPAM gestures for drink. EILIDH looks skeptical so WÂPAM takes a sip first. EILIDH takes a tentative sip, and then drinks the whole container full. She gives back the container.

EILIDH: Thank you.

WÂPAM: tanita itohtêyân? *[Where are you going?]*

EILIDH shakes her head.

EILIDH: I don't understand.

WÂPAM: mwâc ota kakî pâpêyakôyan. *[You shouldn't be out here by yourself.]*

WÂPAM uses gestures as best as they can.

tanita itohteyan? *[Where are you going?]*

EILIDH: That way . . .

EILIDH points north.

I have to go . . . my family . . .

EILIDH exits. WÂPAM watches for a moment, then gets an idea and runs off. The MOON changes the scene slightly and EILIDH re-enters. WÂPAM catches up to EILIDH, they have cranberries in their hand. WÂPAM holds them out and eats one.

WÂPAM: mîcisiw. *[Eat.]*

They give the rest of the berries to EILIDH.

EILIDH: I am hungry . . .

EILIDH rubs her belly then takes one. They are sour, but she eats them all gratefully then goes and picks some berries herself. These berries are from a bush honeysuckle, so WÂPAM hits them out of her hand.

WÂPAM: mwâc! piscipowin. *[No! Poisonous.]*

EILIDH: What?

WÂPAM: piscipowiniwin. *[Poisonous.]*

WÂPAM mimes choking and falling over dead.

EILIDH: Oh. Poisonous.

EILIDH points at the plant and shakes her head, puts her hand over her mouth to indicate she won't eat them. WÂPAM looks confused. EILIDH repeats WÂPAM's mime of choking and falling over dead. She embellishes it a bit. WÂPAM laughs and nods.

WÂPAM: Poisonous.

WÂPAM gets two more berries. EILIDH looks questioningly and gives a bit of the falling over dead gesture. WÂPAM eats one and gives the other to EILIDH.

wâpahta. nipiya kahkinaw mîskocinakôsiwak. cîst-kanawapahta. *[See. The leaves are different. You need to look.]*

WÂPAM points to the different plants, showing the leaves and doing either the hungry belly gesture or the falling over dead gesture, much abbreviated.

EILIDH: Different plants, I get it.

WÂPAM: **ôma mâ?** *[And this one?]*

EILIDH looks at the poisonous plant and gives the poisonous gesture. Then she picks from the cranberry plant and shares with WÂPAM.

(nodding) **tapwê!** *[Yes!]*

EILIDH: Thank you. I need to go.

WÂPAM: **mwâc. nêtê isi.** *[No. That way.]*

EILIDH: What?

WÂPAM: **ana mihcêt pîkiskwêwina kâ âyamit, kiskênihtâm kâ isi âyamiyân, êkwa kakî kiskênitnaw kêkwan ohci pêyakoyân ota nôhcimihk.** *[The one who speaks many languages, they know yours, and we can find out why you are alone in the woods.]*

EILIDH looks puzzled, WÂPAM tries to mime their camp. EILIDH shakes her head. WÂPAM tries gently guiding EILIDH the way to the camp.

EILIDH shakes her head no.

EILIDH: No. I need to go this way. It's important.

WÂPAM: *(trying English)* No. No.

EILIDH mimes "this way" and starts leaving.

EILIDH: I have to go this way.

WÂPAM pauses while listening, then decisively attempts English.

WÂPAM: Hvvvttto.

EILIDH: Yes. Have to.

WÂPAM: Yeees. Havvvtto.

WÂPAM points to the direction of their family camp.

ni wahkomakanânak. *[My family.]*

EILIDH tries to use gestures.

EILIDH: My parents left me on the boats.

EILIDH gestures.

My mother, my father, my family. They are this way . . . I think.

WÂPAM: ki wahkomakanânak. *[Your family.]*

WÂPAM indicates the direction EILIDH wants to go.

EILIDH: waaaak . . . *[faaammmi . . .]*

Wâpam: ni wahkomakanânak. *[My family.]*

WÂPAM makes a gesture for family and points east.

EILIDH: My **wahkomakanânak** *[family].*

EILIDH points north.

I have to go. They might need my help.

WÂPAM: Help?

EILIDH: Yes, I need to help.

WÂPAM: Help?

EILIDH: Yes.

EILIDH gestures.

My mother is going to have a baby, that is why they left me behind on the boats. Baby. Now. Do you understand?

WÂPAM copies the mother pregnant and going to have a baby gesture. WÂPAM nods. EILIDH has an idea and pulls out her drawing.

EILIDH: See, they are here.

WÂPAM points questioningly to a nearby landmark EILIDH *has drawn.*

Three tall trees *(uses the drawing and gestures)* near a bend in the river.

WÂPAM: hâw. nikiskênitân ita. êkwa mâka. *[Okay. I know this place. Let's go.]*

WÂPAM gestures to go where EILIDH *wants to go.*

MOON: Okânawâpacikêw led the way as the two moved quickly through the forest. **Okânawâpacikêw** knew the land well and understood where Eilidh's drawing said her parents should be. And they were right. The two found Eilidh's parents, her mother still in labour. Her father was surprised to see her.

(acting as Father) "You were supposed to stay on the boats. You were safe there. Why did you come here?"

EILIDH: I couldn't leave my family. I came to help.

WÂPAM: Help? Help? **ni wâhkômâkanak.** *[My family.]*

WÂPAM makes the family gesture.

Help?

WÂPAM makes the birth gesture.

EILIDH: wahkomakanânak means family, I think. Father, do we need help with the birth?

MOON: "Yes . . . help would be good," answered Eilidh's father.

(to WÂPAM, as Father) "Yes, help."

WÂPAM gestures yes and exits.

Okânawâpacikêw soon returned with people from their community to help with the birth.

(as one from WÂPAM's community) **kwâyask kitotân, Okânawâpacikêw.** *[You have done well, Okânawâpacikêw.]*

(to EILIDH) How can we help?

For a while, nothing new happened. Everyone knew it could take time for a baby to be born. Some time passed, and then even more. **Okânawâpacikêw** and Eilidh began to wonder if the baby would ever come . . . until finally . . .

We hear a new baby cry. EILIDH enters carrying the new baby wrapped up. WÂPAM follows.

EILIDH: Hello sister. You are slimy . . . and beautiful. Would you like to hold her?

EILIDH passes the child.

WÂPAM: tanisi nicawasimis. kâ minotakosinin askîhk.
[Hello little child. You have arrived in the world in a good way.]

EILIDH grabs WÂPAM and looks directly into their eyes.

EILIDH: Thank you.

WÂPAM: kîna ohci poko mânimâka. *[You're welcome.]*

EILIDH: *(gestures to herself)* I am Eildih Ruadh McPherson.

WÂPAM: Ay-lee Ra . . .

EILIDH: Call me Eildih. Eilidh.

WÂPAM: **Okânawâpacikêw.**

EILIDH: Okaa . . . okn . . .

WÂPAM: Wâpam. Wâpam.

EILIDH: Thank you, Wâpam.

> *As the MOON speaks, they take a leaf from a tree and make it fall onto the baby. The MOON puppeteers the baby who reacts happily.*

MOON: And so, beside the river with the red water, Eilidh had a baby sister. Her parents named her "one from the river." In Gaelic that name is Struana.

Act Two
The River Freezes

Scene One: Calm

During this, we see the different directions that WÂPAM *and* EILIDH *went on a map of Manitoba.*

MOON: Not long after Struana's birth, Wâpam and their family left and continued their journey north as they did every fall, to reach the wooded land of the muskrat and muskeg. Over the cold months they hunted and trapped many animals including **wapôs** and **môswa**, which means rabbit and moose, harvesting the meat and making clothing of the hides.

Eilidh and her family followed the Red River south. The cold weather waited just long enough for them to clear a bit of land near **ita kâ mâwacîtonâniwâk**, the Meeting Place, and build a sod hut with one room before the river froze smooth and solid.

As the wind blew blankets of snow across the frozen ground, Eilidh and Wâpam each spent time wondering about the other.

Finally, after many months, the ice on the river melted, grew thin and floated away in pieces. Eilidh's family learned which spring plants were good to eat and what seed to put in the soil near the river. Wâpam's family took down their homes and started their journey south, as they did every year, collecting medicines as they returned to the Meeting Place near where Eilidh's family had settled.

EILIDH: Wâpam! You found me! I am so happy to see you again.

WÂPAM: Eilidh.

> *They are both a bit unsure as to how to greet each other but end up in a big hug.*

For you and **ki wahkomakanâk** *[your family]*.

> *WÂPAM hands EILIDH a small bag with medicine in it.*

EILIDH: This is beautiful. How do I say "thank you"?

WÂPAM: Thank you. **êkosanî.** *[Thank you.]*

EILIDH: *(tentatively)* **êkosanî.** *[Thank you.]*

WÂPAM: **kîna ohci poko mânimâka.** *[You're welcome.]*

EILIDH: You wouldn't believe how cold it was this winter. Well, I guess you had winter too, but anyway, it's perfect you came back! Today is my birthday.

WÂPAM: Birthday?

> *EILIDH uses the gesture for "birth" from Act One.*

EILIDH: Birth . . . day. Today I am twelve years old.

EILIDH starts making lines, counting in English and indicates WÂPAM to join.

One, two . . .

EILIDH indicates for WÂPAM to join. WÂPAM counts with EILIDH as she creates the lines and counts in English.

One, two, three, four, five, six, seven, eight, nine, ten, eleven, twelve . . .

WÂPAM: pêyak, nîso, nisto, nêwo, nîyânan, nikotwâsik, têpakohp, ayênânêw, kêkâc-mitâtaht, mitâtaht, pêya-kosâp, nîsosâp. *[One, two, three, four, five, six, seven, eight, nine, ten, eleven, twelve.]*

EILIDH: I am twelve today.

WÂPAM nods and gestures "birth."

WÂPAM: I was birth . . . twelve **mihkowi-pîsimôhk ispîhk** *[during a blood moon].* **mihkow.** *[Red.]*

WÂPAM shows EILIDH something red.

mihkow. *[Red.]*

EILIDH: Red.

WÂPAM: Yes. Red. I was birth.

EILIDH: Born.

WÂPAM: Yes. Born . . . red **tipiskawi-pîsim** *[moon].*

WÂPAM gestures to the red object, then gestures "moon."

EILIDH: Wait. **pîsim** *[moon/month]* means moon, right? Twelve years ago, born under a red moon, a blood moon?

WÂPAM: Yes.

EILIDH: Wâpam, me too! I can't believe it. We have the same birthday! Happy birthday!

WÂPAM: Happy birthday.

EILIDH smells the bag.

EILIDH: This smells lovely. What is inside?

WÂPAM: maskihkî. *[Medicines.]*

EILIDH: maskihkî? *[Medicines?]*

WÂPAM: Yes. Medicines. From **ni wahkomakanânak** *[my family]* to you.

EILIDH: Thank your family for me.

MOON: During this summer, Wâpam's family came by to see how the little baby born by the river had grown, and to show Eilidh's family how to use the medicines Wâpam gave them. Eilidh worked with her family as they planted their food and built a log home.

We see this happening.

Wâpam visited often, helping and learning the language of the settlers.

WÂPAM picks up STRUANA *and spins, we hear a giggle.*

Struana always giggled when Wâpam would pick her up and spin her in circles.

Scene Two: Promises

September

WÂPAM carries a basket of red berries.

WÂPAM: **maskêkominâna.** *[Cranberries.]*

EILIDH: *(tries Cree)* **maasgeg . . . msaageg . . .** *[crann . . . cannn . . .]* I remember those!

WÂPAM: **maskêkominâna.** *[Cranberries.]*

EILIDH attempts a few more times unsuccessfully than gets it close.

EILIDH: **maskêkominâna.** *[Cranberries.]*

WÂPAM: **tapwê!** *[Yes!]*

WÂPAM tosses a cranberry to Eilidh, who nearly catches it in her mouth but misses.

EILIDH: You are so much better at languages than me.

WÂPAM: I have been practising with **ana mihcet pîkiskwêwina ka ayamit.** The one who speaks many languages.

EILIDH: Try again. I'll get it this time.

WÂPAM tosses another cranberry, this time a bit too far.

WÂPAM: Again?

WÂPAM holds up another cranberry.

EILIDH: Go.

The two get into "ready" positions and WÂPAM tosses a third cranberry, and EILIDH catches it this time. WÂPAM tosses one up in the air to themselves.

EILIDH: Oh! I made something for you.

She shows WÂPAM a drawing on birch bark parchment.

See, it's the house!

WÂPAM: Yes, I see.

EILIDH: So you have something to remember it when you are away on the land with no house. Isn't it great?

WÂPAM: I have a house, just different.

EILIDH: I know. But isn't it cold in the winter?

WÂPAM: No, it's nice and warm.

EILIDH: How?

WÂPAM: There are lots of ways we keep warm. We build fires, like you do, and we use the furs from the animals we hunt.

EILIDH gives WÂPAM the drawing.

Thank you. You are better at—

    WÂPAM gestures.

EILIDH: Drawing?

WÂPAM: Yes, drawing.

EILIDH: I draw a lot.

WÂPAM: It is time for us to go north.

    EILIDH sighs.

EILIDH: I wish you could stay.

WÂPAM: We will be back when the ice melts and the leaves return to the trees.

EILIDH: I will miss you.

WÂPAM: What is miss?

EILIDH: Miss. Uh . . . you know.

    EILIDH hugs them.

I want you to stay.

WÂPAM: You should come. Come with me and my family.

EILIDH: That would be lovely! I want to learn how to use a bow and arrow.

WÂPAM: I can teach you how.

EILIDH: And you should stay. One winter, stay here with us. We can talk all winter long. And I can teach you how to use a spindle!

WÂPAM: I would need to think on it. It would be different.

EILIDH: It would be fun!

WÂPAM: Yes. Yes! I could stay.

EILIDH: Promise?

> *EILIDH holds out her hand to shake on it.*

WÂPAM: Promise?

EILIDH: It means something you must do. Something you cannot break.

WÂPAM: If I say it, I will do it. So what is promise?

EILIDH: It's a deal. It means we agree. You promise to stay with me and my family over one winter.

WÂPAM: And you promise to come on the land with me. Yes. Promise.

> *WÂPAM takes EILIDH's hands. EILIDH moves the hands up and down. WÂPAM follows enthusiastically and takes it bit too far.*

EILIDH: Right. Yes. Enough! You take your handshake seriously. Wâpam, you can let go now.

Scene Three: The Problem with Sheep

July

MOON: The two spoke of the unbreakable promise every time Wâpam's family came to the meeting place. They also talked about their very different lives.

> *EILIDH has* STRUANA *(twenty-two months old) on her lap in a pile of blankets. The* MOON *puppeteers* STRUANA *who is sleeping and then stirs.*

EILIDH: Shhh . . . sleep. Sleep.

WÂPAM: So at your home across the ocean . . . they burned everything?

EILIDH: Yes, everything. All the fields, all the houses. Everything. We were warned, so we left before that happened.

WÂPAM: Why would someone want to burn everything?

EILIDH: To make room for sheep.

WÂPAM: For sheep?

EILIDH: Yes. Sheep.

> *EILIDH throws a sheepskin over her head and says "Baaa."* WÂPAM *laughs.*

WÂPAM: Like the farmers here. Always killing the buffalo that break the fences. Buffalo don't understand fences . . .

Eilidh: No, they don't.

WÂPAM: Why would they want so many sheep? To feed coyotes?

WÂPAM gets down on their hands and knees and starts baaing like a sheep.

Baaa, baaaaaaa.

EILIDH: Shhhh . . . you will wake Struana. Don't make me laugh.

WÂPAM: Baaa, baaa—oh no, a coyote! Don't eat me! Ahhh-harg, owww!

EILIDH is trying not to laugh.

EILIDH: No, stop. Struana is so grumpy if she doesn't have her nap.

WÂPAM continues the gory death, mimicking the poisonous death gesture from Act One.

Wâpam. Stop.

STRUANA stirs again.

WÂPAM: Shh shh shh, sleep.

STRUANA settles.

She looks . . . peaceful.

Beat.

Did you ask yet?

EILIDH: Ask what?

WÂPAM: To come stay with me.

WÂPAM grabs EILIDH's hand and shakes it.

EILIDH: Wâpam, we do not need to shake hands every time we talk about our promise. I'm sure I can come stay with you. After all, your family helped with Struana's birth. When Struana is older, I'm sure I can come.

WÂPAM: And I will stay. While I am here, I can teach you snares. Then you will be ready to stay with me and my family.

EILIDH: I can't wait.

WÂPAM: Ask.

EILIDH: I will.

WÂPAM: Ask soon.

EILIDH: Don't worry, I will. When the time is right.

Scene Four: Staying

July

MOON: Wâpam and Eilidh remained good friends, even as they followed different cycles and learned different things. Wâpam's family again left for the woods in the north and Eilidh's family stayed as the river froze. **wîpac takwâhkin:** early fall, **ati âhkwatin:** freeze-up, **pipon:** winter, **wîpac pê sîkwan:** early spring, **kâ sîkwâhk:** spring. As the grass grew green and the trees became full with leaves, Wâpam's family returned. And Struana, the little one from the river, grew and grew. She was almost three years old.

STRUANA is hiding with EILIDH's spinning.

EILIDH: *(off stage)* Struana!?!

STRUANA pops her head out to see if EILIDH is coming. She giggles and hides again. She is holding a hand spindle. EILIDH enters.

Struana, come out right now. Where are you?

EILIDH looks around then goes to look off stage. STRUANA pops her head out looking for EILIDH. WÂPAM enters.

EILIDH: *(off stage)* Struana, come out! If you unravel my thread, I will be angry.

WÂPAM sneaks up on STRUANA and picks her up.

MOON: *(as STRUANA)* Wâpam!!

WÂPAM swings STRUANA in a circle, she laughs.

WÂPAM: You are not so little, **nicawasimis** *[little one]*. You are getting bigger.

MOON: Spin!

WÂPAM spins STRUANA again.

EILIDH: *(while entering)* Struana, I give up, get out here . . . Wâpam!

EILIDH gives WÂPAM a hug while STRUANA is still in their arms.

You're back. Finally!

WÂPAM: We just arrived.

EILIDH: You have to tell me everything! I mean, how was the—

MOON: *(as STRUANA)* Spin!

> *WÂPAM takes the hand spindle from STRUANA and hands it back to EILIDH.*

WÂPAM: Is this yours?

EILIDH: Yes. Thank you. Struana, go tell our parents Wâpam is here.

MOON: *(as STRUANA)* Spin!

EILIDH: Struana. I said go tell Mother. I'm sure that she and Father will want to say hello to Wâpam.

> *STRUANA stands, hesitating. She doesn't want to go.*

WÂPAM: Listen to your sister. We can play later.

> *STRUANA leaves.*

EILIDH: How was the winter? The ice was so smooth this year. And the cold lasted way too long. Oh, what new thing did you learn? Tell me everything! You always seem to learn something big every year. Hey, look at this thread! I finally can get it mostly even.

WÂPAM: Slow down, Eilidh. Yes, the thread is nice, and it was a very good winter.

EILIDH: I missed you.

WÂPAM: I missed you too. Struana is getting big. Do you think she is old enough now? For you to leave and come stay with me?

EILIDH: Maybe. Yes, I think she is.

WÂPAM: Then we will not have to be apart for a long time! My family says I can stay here this winter, and the winter after you can come with us.

EILIDH: You don't have to go north?

WÂPAM: I will stay with you and your family, practise my English, and learn your ways of living. And I have so much I can show you. Then you will be ready to be with my family on the land.

EILIDH: This is wonderful!!

WÂPAM: Yes it is. Have you asked yet?

STRUANA peeks around a corner.

MOON: *(as STRUANA)* Wâpam! Come on!

WÂPAM: I had better go see what she wants.

EILIDH: Welcome back, Wâpam. And welcome home!

MOON: At the arrival of the Falling Leaf Moon, Wâpam's ô wâhkômâkanak [their family] left to head north, as they always do. But this time, instead of going with them, Wâpam stayed at the farm with Eilidh and her family. The air grew colder, and the water falling from the sky transformed from rain into snow. As the Wolf Moon rose, the bitter winds blew the blankets of white across the frozen ground.

Scene Five: Cracking

January

> EILIDH is carding wool, WÂPAM is checking the knots on snares. STRUANA is sleeping.

EILIDH: What are you doing?

WÂPAM: I am just fixing her knots.

EILIDH: Whose knots?

WÂPAM: Struana's. I am teaching her how to make a snare.

EILIDH: Why? She's too young for that.

WÂPAM: I learned how to snare rabbits and marten when I was her age. I can teach you instead if you want.

EILIDH: Maybe later.

WÂPAM: Struana is very good with her hands. And she wants to learn.

EILIDH: She needs to learn the skills we need here.

WÂPAM: But this is important too.

EILIDH: It is different here from the way your family lives.

WÂPAM: I know.

EILIDH: I haven't seen you working on your spinning. How's it going?

   WÂPAM is quiet for a moment.

WÂPAM: I will get to it.

EILIDH: Do you want me to show you how to do it again?

WÂPAM: No, I know how, but I've been / working on this new—

EILIDH: You came to learn.

WÂPAM: I have been learning. The language comes much easier to me now. But I miss helping the young ones with their snares. And I miss being outside. You stay inside so much more here.

EILIDH: Because it's freezing out there!

WÂPAM: Maybe it feels colder because you don't go outside. I don't feel so cold when I am with my family during **mikisi-wi-pîsim** *[February]*, the Eagle Moon.

EILIDH: We agreed to practise calendar months, remember?

WÂPAM: The months do not describe the time as well as the moons. It is just some word with no meaning.

EILIDH: To you. I'm sure it has meaning . . . in some language. I don't know what it is.

WÂPAM: See? Why do you follow it if you do not know what it means? We call it **pinâskawi-pîsim** [October]. Falling Leaf Moon is just a much better way to describe the beginning of the fifth season.

EILIDH: There are only four / seasons.

WÂPAM: I know there are only four seasons in English. I need to know how to communicate between many peoples. And I do. I know how to translate fall into either **wîpac takwâkin** [early fall] or **ati âhkwatin** [freeze-up] depending on if they are speaking about fall or (searching for the word) freeze-up.

    STRUANA begins to stir.

EILIDH: Shhh. Just sleep a little more.

    STRUANA sits up groggily.

No, not yet. Go back to sleep.

WÂPAM: Shhh. Sleep now, **nipa, nicawasimis** [sleep, little one].

    STRUANA lays back down. They both watch carefully.

EILIDH: Even half asleep, she still listens to you better. Here.

    EILIDH hands one of the paddles to WÂPAM and they begin carding together.

Scene Six: Dreams of Ice

> *It is laundry day.* EILIDH *brings out a washboard in the large wooden washtub.*

WÂPAM & MOON: *(MOON as STRUANA)* **pêyak** *[one]*, **nîso** *[two]*, **nisto** *[three]*, jump. **nêwo** *[four]*, **nîyânan** *[five]*, **nikotwâsik** *[six]*, jump.

> STRUANA *sits down to the side fiddling with a snare.* WÂPAM *goes to join* EILIDH *at the washtub.*

EILIDH: *(gently teasing)* Okay Wâpam, let's see if you can get this stain out.

> WÂPAM *goes to the washboard.*

Be careful with your knuckles on the washboard this time.

WÂPAM: Oh don't worry. I won't make that mistake again.

EILIDH: Well, at least Struana was able to learn that lesson without hurting herself. Now she knows too. Right, Struana?

MOON: *(as STRUANA)* Yes! Thanks, Wâpam.

WÂPAM: You're welcome, Struana.

EILIDH: She's very careful with the washboard now.

> *A pause as* WÂPAM *washes.*

WÂPAM: I saw **ni wâhkômâkanak** *[my family]* last night.

EILIDH: Your family? How?

WÂPAM: While I was sleeping.

EILIDH: That is called—

WÂPAM: Dreaming. I remember.

EILIDH: You dream much more than I do. And when I do dream, I hardly remember them.

WÂPAM: Nohkôm [*Grandmother*] told me once that when people visit us in our sleep, they are thinking about us. I hope they are. I miss **ni wâhkômâkanak** [*my family*].

EILIDH: What was the dream this time?

WÂPAM: We were sitting around a fire **Nohkôm** [*Grandmother*] made. We were listening to her tell a story. I looked across the fire at **Nimosôm** [*Grandfather*] and he smiled at me. I can still see his face so clearly.

MOON: (*as STRUANA, holding up a snare*) It's broken.

WÂPAM: Here, let me see. Let's make that one a bit tighter.

WÂPAM dries their hands and goes to STRUANA.

EILIDH: We can be your family, you know. Me and Struana.

WÂPAM: Yes. I know. Your parents have been very kind to me. That one there, see how you missed a step. We need to put the wire through that.

MOON: (*as STRUANA*) It's still broken!

EILIDH: Struana, don't worry about it, you don't need to learn that. Come help with the laundry.

MOON: *(as STRUANA)* I want to fix it.

WÂPAM: Wait, we need to look more closely / at that . . .

Eilidh: Hey! Someone needs to help me. Struana, come here.

MOON: *(as STRUANA, to WÂPAM)* Like this?

EILIDH: Struana, you have to learn to listen to your older sister. When Father and Mother aren't here, I'm in charge.

WÂPAM: Maybe it's the way you talk to her. Try a different way.

EILIDH: She just needs to listen. That's all.

WÂPAM: You keep working, **nicawasimis** *[little one]*. I'll go help with the laundry.

> *WÂPAM pats STRUANA's head.*

Scene Seven: Breaking Ice

February

MOON: That year, the water was high and quick moving beneath the ice as it cracked and shifted leaving jagged pieces scattered across the surface, which made the ice looked damaged and scarred.

> *STRUANA is busy working on a snare. EILIDH grabs a pail and pours the contents into the soup pot.*

MOON: (*as STRUANA*) Spin?

EILIDH: No, we can't spin right now, Struana.

WÂPAM enters in full winter gear with a water pail.

WÂPAM: This should be the last one.

EILIDH takes the pail and pours it into the soup pot.

MOON: (*as STRUANA*) Spin?

WÂPAM: Of course, **nicawasimis** *[little one]*!

WÂPAM spins STRUANA in a circle and STRUANA giggles.

MOON: (*as STRUANA*) Again!

WÂPAM does it again.

WÂPAM: You are getting bigger, **nicawasimis** *[little one]*.

MOON: (*as STRUANA*) Again!

EILIDH: She never tires of that.

WÂPAM: Struana, I need to get all this off. Then we can do it again.

STRUANA begins pulling winter wear off WÂPAM to help speed up the process. This gets WÂPAM tangled up.

WÂPAM: Slow down. Woah, wait / not that way.

EILIDH: Struana, woah, slow / down.

WÂPAM: Hold on. Watch out.

WÂPAM ends up in a pile on the ground with STRUANA on top of them trying to pull winter gear off.

Ouch.

EILIDH: Struana, stop.

She removes STRUANA and puts her down on one of the snares. EILIDH tries to help WÂPAM. WÂPAM is so wound up in outerwear, it is difficult for WÂPAM to stand.

The next lines are overlapping.

No, go that way. Not that way. This way. Other way. No. Turn.

WÂPAM: Ouch. That does not work. Wait. I can do it! Let me go.

Both end up a bit breathless and laughing by the end.

EILIDH: Well that . . . happened.

STRUANA holds up her arm with a snare on it.

MOON: *(as STRUANA)* Wâpam? The snare is stuck.

EILIDH: Oh no, Struana, let me help.

WÂPAM: You can't pull there, Eilidh. Struana, you know how to loosen it. Remember.

EILIDH: What? Wâpam, just get it off her.

MOON: *(as STRUANA)* I . . . I . . . pull on the . . .

EILIDH: Just get it off her. Now.

WÂPAM: Just wait. She can do this.

EILIDH: I'm serious. She's just a child. Get that thing off her.

MOON: *(as STRUANA)* First pull on the circle cord.

WÂPAM: Right. Then on the . . .

MOON: *(as Struana)* Straight cord.

WÂPAM: Yes.

> *The snare comes off.* EILIDH *checks on* STRUANA'*s arm.*

EILIDH: Are you okay?

MOON: *(as STRUANA)* I'm okay.

EILIDH: She could have really hurt herself.

WÂPAM: But she didn't. She remembered.

EILIDH: It's too dangerous for her.

WÂPAM: No it isn't. I learned when I was her age. She is learning how to use it safely.

EILIDH: What if she gets stuck again and no one is around?

WÂPAM: If it happens again, she knows how to get out of it.

EILIDH: She doesn't need to know how to get out of these snares. She doesn't need to know how to build them, she doesn't need them at all!

MOON: (*as STRUANA*) I like making snares.

EILIDH: It does not matter what you like. Right now, you do what Mother, Father, and I tell you to do.

WÂPAM: Eilidh, there is so much that I could teach you both. Why won't you let me?

EILIDH: Why can't you just be like us?

WÂPAM: I do not want to become you. I am **maskêko-ininiwak** [*Swampy Cree*].

EILIDH: But you can be so much more than that!

WÂPAM goes still and silent.

You could learn to farm or work at the fort as an interpreter. You could have a house.

WÂPAM: I don't need a house. I have a home. I am proud of my family. That is who I am and who I want to be.

EILIDH: I'm not trying to insult you or your family . . . I'm just saying that now there is another option for you.

WÂPAM: Why is being **maskêko-ininiwak** [*Swampy Cree*] not enough?

EILIDH: Don't you see you can be so much more than that?

WÂPAM: What I see is you don't value my way of life. I see you want to change me.

EILIDH: Yes, because you can be something here.

WÂPAM: I am something. I showed you the way in the forest. And now I am not good enough.

EILIDH: Wâpam—

WÂPAM gets up. STRUANA falls off their lap.

WÂPAM: *(yelling)* I am more than good enough!

MOON: *(as STRUANA)* Why are you yelling?

WÂPAM: I'm sorry, **nicawasimis** *[little one]*.

EILIDH: It's okay, Struana. We won't yell anymore.

MOON: *(as STRUANA)* Are you angry? What's wrong?

WÂPAM: Yes, I am angry. But it will be okay, **nicawasimis** *[little one]*. It will be okay.

EILIDH goes back to the soup. WÂPAM snuggles STRUANA.

Scene Eight: Shattered

A new day. WÂPAM is folding laundry when EILIDH comes in holding a drawing she has made.

EILIDH: A present for you. It's the three of us.

WÂPAM: We look good.

EILIDH hands it to WÂPAM. STRUANA looks at it.

EILIDH: I made it with—

WÂPAM: wapôs *[rabbit].*

EILIDH: Yes, rabbit skin. I wanted it to last.

WÂPAM: Thank you.

MOON: *(as STRUANA)* **môswa** *[moose]* nose.

WÂPAM turns the drawing on its side.

WÂPAM: môswa *[moose]* nose? . . . Wait. Does my nose really look like that?

EILIDH: Like what?

STRUANA looks sideways at WÂPAM and the drawing.

MOON: *(as STRUANA)* Moose nose.

EILIDH: I didn't mean to make your nose look like a moose.

EILIDH gives WÂPAM something to see their reflection.

WÂPAM: But a moose has a . . . oh. I guess I can see that a bit. Maybe.

MOON: *(as STRUANA)* **môswa** *[moose]* nose. Moose nose!

WÂPAM: If you told **Nimosôm** *[Grandfather]*, it would stay with me forever. One time, **Nohkôm** *[Grandmother]* got food stuck in her teeth. **Nimosôm** *[Grandfather]* saw and still calls her **kâ sêkotâpitêt**. It means food stuck in teeth.

MOON: *(as STRUANA)* **kâ sêkotâpitêt.** *[Food stuck in teeth.]*

WÂPAM: That's it! I miss them. **Nimosôm** *[Grandfather]* is so funny. When you come with me, you will see.

> STRUANA *goes to* WÂPAM *and snuggles on their lap.* EILIDH *looks uncomfortable.*

EILIDH: I can't go.

WÂPAM: What do you mean?

EILIDH: Next winter. I can't go.

WÂPAM: Then you can come the winter after.

EILIDH: No. I can't go, ever.

WÂPAM: Why not? Struana is old enough. You said so.

EILIDH: I know. It isn't because of Struana.

WÂPAM: Is it your parents?

EILIDH: They won't let me go.

WÂPAM: Why not? What did they say?

> EILIDH *is quiet.*

Did you even ask them?

EILIDH: No, I don't have to. I know what they would say.

WÂPAM: How do you know for sure? My family said yes.

EILIDH: That is different.

WÂPAM: My family helped your family when you were in the woods. Your parents have more reason to say yes.

EILIDH: Fine. I don't want to go.

WÂPAM: But what about our promise? We agreed I would stay here and then you would come with my family.

EILIDH: But that was before.

WÂPAM: I am here. Doing what I said I would. Now it's your turn.

> *WÂPAM holds out their hand to shake. EILIDH looks at it but doesn't take it.*

WÂPAM: You promised.

EILIDH: I know.

WÂPAM: You can't break your promise.

> *EILIDH takes WÂPAM's hand in both of her hands.*

EILIDH: I know! It's just that now you're here and can see how great life is on the farm. The world is changing. You need to change too. Stay in one place and have a home.

STRUANA nudges WÂPAM, trying to play.

WÂPAM: I have a home. I have **ni wahkomakanânak** *[my family]*. I don't need a wooden building to tell me who I am or where I belong.

EILIDH: What's wrong with our home? I thought you liked it here.

WÂPAM gets up, leaving STRUANA on the chair.

WÂPAM: You get me to stay here with the promise that next you will join my family. And now you are not coming. I have tried to teach you what I know but you aren't willing to learn anything.

Beat.

You tricked me.

EILIDH: I did not. Do you really expect me to leave my home—

WÂPAM: Yes.

EILIDH: And my family to go—

WÂPAM: I did.

EILIDH: Yes, but you came here. Where life is better.

WÂPAM stands up.

WÂPAM: *(yelling)* Life is different. Not better.

STRUANA hides behind WÂPAM.

MOON: *(as STRUANA)* Stop fighting!

EILIDH: Struana, put down that snare and come over here.

WÂPAM: *(to STRUANA)* I'm sorry for yelling, **nicawasimis** [*little one*].

EILIDH: Struana, put that snare down, carefully . . .

WÂPAM: The snare isn't dangerous.

EILIDH: Struana, come over here.

> STRUANA *holds onto* WÂPAM *tighter.*

WÂPAM: If you kept your promise, if you came out on the land, you would understand.

EILIDH: I don't want to keep my promise, I don't want to learn about the snares or the land! Why can't you see how much better this life is?

WÂPAM: I do see. I see this life is a broken promise.

EILIDH: Struana, I said come over here.

MOON: *(as STRUANA)* No!

> EILIDH *goes over and picks up a squirming* STRUANA.

EILIDH: Struana, that is enough.

WÂPAM: Eilidh, you are scaring her.

EILIDH: I am not, she just needs to listen to me.

WÂPAM: Eilidh, stop.

EILIDH: You. You stay away from my sister.

> *EILIDH whips STRUANA out of the MOON's hands, leaving the puppet still and the MOON's hands in the air, empty. EILIDH exits with STRUANA. WÂPAM is left reeling, watching where EILIDH and STRUANA just were. Slowly WÂPAM leaves. The MOON looks at her hands left in the air and then looks at the audience. Underneath, there is a sound like ice cracking and breaking.*

Act Three
The River Thaws

Scene One: Frozen Water

Present day. A blood moon returns.

MOON: Sometimes we get so lost in our own world or so scared of someone else's that we fail to see clearly. We hurt people. We freeze like the river, jagged and dangerous.

Wâpam returned to their family. Eilidh refused to see that both of their lives, as different as they may be, have value and purpose. The two never spoke again after that winter. I watched and waited for them to reunite . . . but they never did.

So we move forward in time. The river has become just an obstacle for the new concrete highways. Boats become trains, then cars, then planes, and everything moves so fast. It is easy to forget how to listen; how to really see.

About eleven years ago, almost to the day, it happened again. Two babies were born, under a blood moon, in a small town near the place Wâpam and Eilidh broke apart. In the province some call Manitoba, in the country some call Canada. These little ones didn't cry, not because they couldn't or because there's anything wrong with crying, but because one was busy doing and the other was busy seeing . . . sound familiar?

Scene Two: Water Woes

A modern school, outside the main office. There is a bench and a tank with a turtle inside puppeteered by the MOON.

WÂPAM enters with a backpack and a tattered book in their hand. They greet the turtle.

WÂPAM: tapwê mino-wapan o Wîtimikwânisiw. *[Good morning, Turtle.]*

They grab a seat on the bench, sighing heavily. They begin to read. EILIDH *enters with a huge yawn. She looks around for somewhere to sit, then takes a seat on the other end of the bench, closer to the tank.*

Looking around, she notices the turtle. EILIDH *puts her hand on the glass, drawing back one finger, about to tap on the glass when* WÂPAM *clears their throat loudly.*

EILIDH: What?

WÂPAM: Look.

WÂPAM chin-points to the sign taped on the side of the tank that clearly says: "PLEASE DON'T TAP THE GLASS." EILIDH *stops.*

EILIDH: Don't tap the . . . Whoops.

EILIDH sighs.

This sucks . . . how is there still forty minutes until first bell? No one is here this early.

wâpam: I'm here.

eilidh: Well, except you. And me. And this turtle.

wâpam: O Wîtimikwânisiw. *[Turtle.]*

eilidh: Huh?

wâpam: O Wîtimikwânisiw. *[Turtle.]* The turtle's name in **maskeko-Ininiwak** *[Swampy Cree].*

eilidh: Wittttiimm—

wâpam: O Wîtimikwânisiw. *[Turtle.]*

eilidh: Oh. That's kinda hard to say.

wâpam: Not really. It means turtle in Swampy Cree.

eilidh: Well, it's hard to remember.

wâpam: No it's not.

eilidh: Fine. But I think I'll stick with turtle.

wâpam: What? The name is too hard, so you just decide not to learn it?

eilidh: Whoa. Sorry.

> *Beat.*

I don't think I have seen you around before. Are you new here?

WÂPAM: Nope. I've been coming here since grade one.

EILIDH: Really? Then why haven't I seen you around much?

WÂPAM: I dunno.

EILIDH: I'm Eilidh, by the way.

WÂPAM: Yeah, I know who you are. I'm Wâpam. You're in Ms. Quarter's class. I'm in Mr. Waning's.

EILIDH: Oh, no way! My friend Hayley is in your class.

WÂPAM: She's nice. We don't talk much though.

EILIDH: So . . . why are you here so early?

WÂPAM: This is when the bus drops us off.

EILIDH: What bus?

WÂPAM: The bus from the rez.

EILIDH: I didn't even know a bus came to the school this early. Why don't you just walk instead?

> WÂPAM *looks up at* EILIDH.

WÂPAM: Do you know where the reserve is?

EILIDH: Kinda, but I haven't been there.

WÂPAM: It's like a forty-minute bus ride.

EILIDH: . . . Oh. Then why do you come here?

WÂPAM: This is the closest school.

EILIDH: That sucks. I like not having to wake up early all the time.

WÂPAM: I would too.

EILIDH: It's nice to sleep in.

WÂPAM: Yeah.

EILIDH: My mom dropped me off early today because she wanted to go to her gym before work to take a shower. We have no water at home.

No response.

I'm sure you've heard about the frozen pipes.

WÂPAM: The what?

EILIDH: Frozen pipes! It's awful.

WÂPAM: No, I didn't hear.

EILIDH: What? How? All the houses on my street have frozen pipes.

WÂPAM: That sucks.

EILIDH: Do you have water at your house?

WÂPAM: Yeah . . . but—

EILIDH: Lucky. I can hardly remember what it was like . . .

WÂPAM: How long has it been?

EILIDH: Forever! It's been like four days.

WÂPAM: Four days!?!

EILIDH: I know right. Each day feels like a lifetime.

WÂPAM: Yeah, but the pipes won't be frozen forever, you will get your running water back.

EILIDH: But who knows how long? My dad told me one time they froze for MONTHS. How could anyone live without water they can just, you know, drink?

WÂPAM: People do. They figure it out.

EILIDH: This is really an outrage, isn't it?

WÂPAM: Whatever.

EILIDH: It is. And I'm going to do something about it.

> WÂPAM *looks up again from their book.*

WÂPAM: What are you gonna do?

EILIDH: I dunno . . . find out who's in charge of the water and write a letter. No . . . we can do better . . . Oh! I know. We can organize a student walkout!

WÂPAM: Hold on, what do you mean "we"?

EILIDH: I'm gonna post this right now—what do you think we need? Three days to organize it? Yeah, three should be enough. There. You wanna see what I posted? You can post something similar if you want.

WÂPAM: What? Wait. No. You just got this idea two seconds ago.

EILIDH: We can figure / it out.

WÂPAM: Stop saying "we"! I'm not involved in this.

>   *WÂPAM starts gathering their belongings.*

This isn't gonna solve it.

EILIDH: How do you know that? Someone once said "be the change you want to be . . . " or something like that. Wâpam, you need to learn to just do it!

WÂPAM: You sound like a commercial for running shoes.

EILIDH: You know what I mean. Great things happen when you get out there and shake things up!

WÂPAM: How do you know what you're doing is actually gonna help?

EILIDH: It will get attention or . . . something. Wait, where are you going?

WÂPAM: You clearly don't know what you're doing.

EILIDH: Then help me.

WÂPAM: I don't want to help you.

EILIDH: Why not?

WÂPAM: I don't see why I should.

EILIDH: I have a right to water.

WÂPAM: Everyone has a right to water, Eilidh. That doesn't mean they'll get it. I'll see you around.

> WÂPAM *heads out, leaving* EILIDH *behind. We see her think about what* WÂPAM *said for a moment.*

Scene Three: Water Drops

> *It's quiet. When they think no one is watching,* WÂPAM *takes* **Wîtimikwânisiw** *out of their tank and lets them walk around on their hand and arm.* EILIDH *enters, carrying a bunch of signs and posters.*

EILIDH: I don't think you're allowed to do that.

> WÂPAM *jumps.*

WÂPAM: It's not hurting anyone.

EILIDH: Don't worry, I won't tell.

WÂPAM: Animals aren't meant to live behind glass their whole lives.

*They watch **Wîtimikwânisiw** walk around. WÂPAM looks at the things EILIDH is carrying.*

WÂPAM: What's all that stuff?

EILIDH: It's for the walkout.

WÂPAM rolls their eyes.

EILIDH: What?? This is important to me!

WÂPAM looks at the top poster and reads it.

WÂPAM: "Leaders of Tomorrow, Frozen in Today"?

EILIDH: Pretty good, huh? I like that one. I've been trying to come up with slogans.

WÂPAM: Whatever.

EILIDH: You're being kinda rude. What's your problem?

WÂPAM: I'm not interested in explaining anything to you.

EILIDH: I don't understand why you think this is such a bad idea. I'm trying to help my whole street, not just me and my family.

WÂPAM: You're rushing in to fix an issue that really isn't a big deal. Your water will come back.

EILIDH: It's been almost a week since we've had water. That isn't right.

WÂPAM: My reserve hasn't had clean water for eighteen years. That isn't right.

EILIDH: What?

WÂPAM: Our water is contaminated. We can't drink it or wash with it.

EILIDH: You don't have water.

WÂPAM: We have water.

EILIDH: But you can't use it?

WÂPAM: We can use it to flush the toilet, but not to drink or shower.

EILIDH: That's awful. Eighteen years? That's longer than we've been alive!

WÂPAM: I know.

EILIDH: Why didn't you say this yesterday?

WÂPAM: Why would I wanna talk about that with someone that isn't listening to anything I'm saying?

EILIDH: Wâpam, I'm sorry. I'll listen.

WÂPAM: When I was younger, I used to get really mad about it, but my **nohkôm** [grandmother] talked to me about it and she helped me understand that it's not an easy fix. There are many things going on underneath that don't have anything to do with water. People have been trying for a long time and still no clean water.

EILIDH: But how do you shower? What happens if you drink it? Do you have to buy bottled water? Sorry. You don't have to answer me. That's messed up . . . I'm sorry. Your community deserves clean water. We need to fix it. Y'know what? Let's change the walkout. We'll make the reserve the main focus.

WÂPAM: Can't you see it's a way bigger issue than that?

EILIDH: It's worth a shot. I'm trying to help.

WÂPAM: This isn't help. This is—you, making it about you. Trying to make yourself feel better.

EILIDH: Alright, then explain the issue to me.

WÂPAM: Oh no, I'm not doing your homework for you.

EILIDH: Okay I'm good at homework. But can you give me some hints? Tell me what I should be looking for?

WÂPAM: I dunno . . . look for things that are already being done. Like, there are already water protectors doing work. Look at Autumn Peltier. She's an Indigenous water protector.

EILIDH: Okay. Thanks.

> *WÂPAM grabs **Wîtimikwânisiw** and puts them back in their tank.*

WÂPAM: There's tons of stuff online about Autumn and her work. Start there.

EILIDH: These people like Autumn Peltier, they're doing things, right? They're making a difference. Why can't I?

WÂPAM: You can. It's just . . . complicated.

The two exit, both thinking about what the other said.

Scene Four: Moonlight

It's another morning at school, a few days have passed. EILIDH enters, tossing her things down on the bench and taking a seat close to the tank.

EILIDH: Hi . . . turtle.

*She addresses **Wîtimikwânisiw**, who moves closer to EILIDH in their tank.*

EILIDH: Witi . . . Witim . . . I know it means turtle . . .

***Wîtimikwânisiw** seems happy to have a new friend. EILIDH doesn't notice WÂPAM come in. WÂPAM is holding a small canister.*

EILIDH: My name is Eilidh. We met a couple days ago, in case you forgot. Do turtles have good memories? . . . **o Witimi . . . Wit—** *[Tuurrr . . . Tuuu—]*

WÂPAM: o Wîtimikwânisiw. *[Turtle.]*

EILIDH: Oh! You're back.

WÂPAM: Just got dropped off.

WÂPAM pulls out the book they were reading before from their backpack and tries to pick up where they left off.

EILIDH: You're later than the other day.

WÂPAM: We were on the bus almost an hour. Snow drifts.

Beat.

WÂPAM slams the book closed.

I hate this book.

EILIDH: Then why are you reading it?

WÂPAM: English assignment.

Beat.

/ How are your frozen pipes?

EILIDH: I cancelled the walkout.

WÂPAM: You did?

EILIDH: Yeah. And yes, our pipes are still frozen.

WÂPAM: That's too bad.

EILIDH: I was really hoping they wouldn't be, on today of all days.

WÂPAM: What's today?

EILIDH: My birthday.

WÂPAM: . . . seriously?

EILIDH: I don't joke about birthdays . . .

WÂPAM: Today's my birthday.

EILIDH: Are you joking?

WÂPAM: I've never met anyone else that's shared a birthday with me before.

EILIDH: Me either. I was supposed to have a party. All my friends were going to come over and make pizzas and decorate cupcakes, but they can't come because of the whole "can't flush the toilet" thing.

WÂPAM: That sucks. I'm sorry.

EILIDH: What are you doing? You're probably having a party, right?

WÂPAM: Some of my family will come for dinner and then usually we go skating on the river.

EILIDH: Did you invite any friends from school?

WÂPAM: My school friends don't come visit.

EILIDH: Why not?

WÂPAM: Probably because we don't live in town.

EILIDH: Oh, maybe.

WÂPAM: You can always have your party another time.

EILIDH: It won't be the same. Today's my birthday. Not tomorrow, not next week, today.

WÂPAM: I guess.

> *WÂPAM approaches the tank while unscrewing the lid of the canister they're holding.*

EILIDH: What are you doing?

WÂPAM: Sometimes I bring a little snack for **o Wîtimikwânisiw** *[Turtle].*

EILIDH: Oh, cool! Can I feed her?

WÂPAM: Sure, go for it.

> *They hold out the canister for EILIDH to put her hand into. EILIDH realizes as soon as she reaches in that she wasn't prepared for what was inside.*

EILIDH: Oh— WHAT IS THAT???

WÂPAM: Mealworms.

EILIDH: You let me touch worms?!

WÂPAM: Mealworms. And you wanted to.

EILIDH: You could've warned me! I thought it would be leaves or grapes or something!

WÂPAM: I was curious to see what you'd do.

*WÂPAM laughs and sticks their hand in the canister, giving some one by one to **Wîtimikwânisiw**, who happily chows down.*

EILIDH: I can't believe I just touched worms.

WÂPAM: Mealworms. They actually become beetles when they get older.

EILIDH: HOW IS THAT ANY BETTER?

WÂPAM: They're called darkling beetles. They can get kinda big. You can find them outside under rocks and stuff.

EILIDH: Why do you know so much about worms and beetles?

WÂPAM: I like them. We're all connected. Humans, animals, plants, bugs . . . all part of the cycle. I did a project on these beetles for science last month. Got an A.

EILIDH: But . . . they're gross. So gross. You can keep those far away from me, thank you very much.

WÂPAM: Suit yourself. **o Wîtimikwânisiw** *[Turtle]* likes them.

WÂPAM puts the empty canister into their backpack.

EILIDH: . . . I looked up Autumn Peltier last night. She's incredible.

WÂPAM: Yeah, she is.

EILIDH: I really am sorry, Wâpam, for not listening to you before . . . I can see why you got so mad at me.

WÂPAM: It's okay. I was already kinda in a bad mood before you came along.

EILIDH: Why?

WÂPAM: Because I hate this book. We were supposed to choose and I was thinking about all the options but by the time I went up, everything good was taken and I got stuck with this.

EILIDH: I don't really look, I just grab something. That doesn't work so well either.

WÂPAM: No, it doesn't. When I see people not thinking things through, I don't trust it. It makes me freak out a little.

EILIDH: I get it.

WÂPAM: It's just not the way I do things.

> *Wîtimikwânisiw does a little twist in their tank, almost like a dance move. The two of them laugh.*

WÂPAM: Did you see that?

> *Wîtimikwânisiw does it again.*

EILIDH: Yeah. What a strange turtle. I mean . . . **o Wîtimikwâ-nisiw** *[Turtle]*.

WÂPAM: You got it!

EILIDH: Finally . . . Hey, I have an idea, maybe I can come out to visit sometime.

WÂPAM: You wanna come to the reserve?

EILIDH: Yeah. I have things I want to learn . . . need to learn. I don't understand how you could go so long without clean water. That doesn't seem fair.

WÂPAM: No, it's not fair.

EILIDH: There must be something I can do.

WÂPAM: Or maybe even something we can do together. My **Nohkôm** [*grandmother*] taught me that doing something without talking to other people, without listening . . . isn't going to do any good.

EILIDH: Maybe your **Nohkôm** [*grandmother*] can explain it to me? I'll listen, I promise.

WÂPAM: She does like talking. I can ask her. What are you doing tonight?

EILIDH: I dunno. Prolly nothing.

WÂPAM: Do you want to come over to my house?

EILIDH: Really?

WÂPAM: Yeah. We can celebrate our birthdays.

EILIDH: Sure, why not? Celebrating together seems like it would be fun.

WÂPAM: I'll have to call my parents and make sure that works for them.

EILIDH: My dad can probably drive us after school, I'll call him at lunch. Oh! And I can bring stuff so we can make our own pizzas! If that won't mess up your family's plans.

WÂPAM: I love pizza.

EILIDH: And I can bring my skates. But fair warning, I'm not very good at skating.

WÂPAM: That's okay, the ice on the river is nice and smooth this year and I can teach you a few things.

EILIDH: That would be great.

WÂPAM: You don't think your parents will mind?

EILIDH: I'm not sure. But I'm pretty good at convincing people, don't you think?

WÂPAM: Yeah, seems like it.

EILIDH: Wanna meet back here at lunch?

WÂPAM: Yeah. Sounds good.

The two smile at each other and walk off.

We hear a soft beat as the MOON *enters, slowly and steadily increasing. It is familiar and begins to shift into the sound of a flowing river.*

MOON: Today, Eilidh keeps the promise made by her great-great-great-great-great-great grandmother seven generations ago. She goes to visit Wâpam and their family. The two share stories and learn about each other's lives so that one day, they can pass that knowledge on. We are all connected, just like the rivers, lakes, and oceans across our Earth.

As I look down on the world today, I see promises being made, promises being kept, promises being broken. Surrounding all of these, I see choices: your choices that can help us today, and the choices that can help our world seven generations from now.

THE END

Acknowledgements

This script would not be possible without the support and gifts of many people who gave their time, energy, and expertise to the creation process. The playwrights would like to thank:

Cameron Robertson (Language Keeper), Alderick Leask (Elder), Angie Cote (Knowledge Keeper), Gail Maurice, Dawnis and the People's Library (Manitoba Indigenous Cultural Education Centre), Tracey Nepinak, Ann Hodges, Debra Zoerb, Pablo Felices-Luna, Katic German, everyone at Manitoba Theatre for Young People, Stephanie Sy, Erica Wilson, Wahsonti:io Kirby, Emily Meadows, Krystle Pederson, Julie Lumsden, Gwen Collins, Mallory James, Kathleen MacLean, Keely McPeek, Julia Davis, Julia Cirillo, Katie Schmidt, and all of the designers who created the amazing world for our play.

Funding and support for the creation and production of the premiere of *Frozen River* were provided by:

The Manitoba Arts Council, the Canada Council for the Arts, Manitoba Theatre for Young People, and Castlemoon Theatre.

We are honoured to have received the 2021 Sharon Enkin Plays for Young People Award.

Michaela Washburn hails from Alberta and is a proud Métis artist of Cree, French, Irish, and English ancestry. Now based in North Bay, Ontario, she feels blessed to be grounded in ceremony and community-based arts in her work with Aanmitaagzi and Big Medicine Studio. An award-winning actor and writer, Washburn has also garnered multiple award nominations, including the 2023 Johanna Metcalf Performing Arts Prize, the Ontario Arts Council Indigenous Arts Award (2021 and 2018), and the K.M. Hunter Artist Award for Theatre (2011). A published author, Michaela's performance and written work has been shared internationally at festivals and theatres in Wales, Aruba, and across Canada and the United States. Her practice spans theatre, film, television, writing, spoken word, clown, improvisation, hosting, workshop facilitation, and stand-up.

Joelle Peters is an award-winning Anishinaabekwe actor/ playwright working in theatre, television, and film and the current artistic director of Native Earth Performing Arts. Her plays include *Niizh*, *Frozen River* (co-written with Michaela Washburn and Carrie Costello), and *do you remember?* Joelle has performed at theatres and festivals across the country, and she can be seen in the hit TV show *Shoresy* (Crave/Hulu) and the film *In Her City* (Raven West Films Ltd.). Joelle has also narrated two audiobooks with Penguin Random House Canada. In 2020, Joelle was selected as the playwriting protege for the Siminovitch Prize by laureate Tara Beagan. In 2021, *Frozen River* received the Sharon Enkin Plays for Young People Award at the annual Tom Hendry Awards. In 2023, the premiere production of *Niizh* was nominated for four Dora Mavor Moore Awards. Keep up with Joelle at joellepeters.ca and on Instagram @joellepeters.jpg.

Carrie Costello has adapted seven children's books into plays for various ages, including *The Paper Bag Princess*, *The Velveteen Rabbit*, *The Snail and the Whale*, and *There's a Mouse in my House*. The latter was produced by Carousel Players in 2009 and 2010. Carrie's next play, *Water Under the Bridge*, was her first historically inspired work, which she co-wrote with Michaela Washburn. This play was produced in 2012 and toured for two years across three provinces. *Torn Through Time*, co-written with Frances Koncan and Cherissa Richards, was produced by Manitoba Theatre for Young People in 2019. Carrie has toured nationally and internationally as a puppeteer. She lives in Winnipeg, Manitoba.